Trauma
to Truth

A journey from recovery to discovery

CONTENTS

This is dedicated to Grace and Kasen
My legacy, my babies, my world
I love you xxx

This is also for all those that did what it took to survive,
managed to survive and sadly those that didn't make it.
To the warriors and the champions of life.

TRAUMA TO TRUTH

From Trauma to Truth is a collection of self-help writing and poetry through my journey from recovery to discovery.

It contains my own personal experience through trauma to my own truth, stepping off the road that was long and bumpy, onto one that has taken me to a sense of freedom. I am still travelling and think I always will be, but I am no longer scared to walk the road or veer off and explore if needed.

I started my journey after my husband left in 2016, or so I thought. I soon realised I was just masking how I was feeling and putting a fake version of myself out there, as to how I thought I should be. So I started the intensive part of my journey when I was 38.. just after our first lockdown started, back in 2020.

It covers everything from childhood trauma, teenage angst, addiction, domestic abuse, grief, loss, but also is a journey of strength, healing, love and self-acceptance.

I endeavour that my voice can give hope, to you the reader, that you are not alone in your experiences and that there can be a way out to a life that is more peaceful and whole.

It is written in no particular order, just as it came up for me at the time, but it is all words from the heart and with love.

It is a book of lessons to encourage, inspire and give hope that amid hardships and trauma, a life can blossom, grow and turn into something strong, resilient and beautiful.

As an added note, most of the content of this book has been written between early 2018 up until the present. early 2023. I am always a work in progress.

LESSON ONE
T is for Trauma

Using the word trauma…

The word trauma is quite a broad-spectrum word. It means different levels of painful experiences to different people. What might be traumatic to one person, may not be to another. It is a very personal experience.

I have often used the word trauma as I have not really wanted to use the actual words of what has happened to me in my 39 years.

I have always been good at minimising what has happened… but this is not a tale of woe…if anything I am stronger and a more rounded person for it.

I got bought up in a violent household, where I would witness my mum being beaten and verbally abused. My earliest memory is of my dad with his hands around my mum's throat, I was 4 years old. Due to my home life, I was a quiet child, painfully shy and this caused me to be bullied throughout primary school. Wincing from going red from embarrassment, even when someone said my name.

There have been pivotal moments of trauma through my life, where I have found myself thinking there is no way back. One of those times is being groomed when I was 15 and being hooked on drugs. I thought it was great having a 29 year old boyfriend, who was a heroin addict, who lied and told me he was clean (this day in age this is grooming and I had a hard time accepting that).

I had pretty much left home at this point, was not attending school, the family had broken down, dad had left and mum was working 3 jobs to keep us afloat. I was left to try and bring up my brother, who was 10.5 at the time. I felt responsibility for things I shouldn't have, like protecting my mum and brother. I had no clue who I was, why I was or what I was doing. I put myself in harm's way many, many times.

I sought out risky behaviours and as the years went by trauma seemed to dominate my life. This was down to feeling the need to people please to avoid confrontation. I experienced several domestically abusive relationships and even got raped. I always wondered why I was getting in these situations, I have since figured out the answer to this question.

It has been a long and arduous journey, but it was down to a sense of wanting to belong and being scared to use my own voice.. because women in my world did not have the right.

I was too fearful to form my own opinions, just falling in line with everyone else. I had been victimising myself and not knowing it.

So that being said, please do not ever minimise your trauma and what it means to you but do not be afraid to dig deep and be courageous, to travel that bumpy road that is full of unknowns and pain, because I talk from experience, It will be worth it in the end.

Trauma clock

Tick tock goes the trauma clock…
Like a timer on a bomb, waiting to cause an explosion
The counter stops, trauma eats away like corrosion
Tick tock goes the trauma clock.
When seconds feel like hours
Hours can feel like days
Time is healer, everyone says.
When they say in time you heal
The hurt gets less
How long does it take? Is anyone's guess.
The hands move slow, sometimes fast
No one can tell you how long this pain will last.
Tick tock goes the trauma clock
When suddenly one day, the clock ….stops….

Salt

Overrun with emotions
Is when my tears turn to oceans
Coming in waves
Raging on for days
The comforting, yet bitter taste of salt
The swell of the currents, wash over in torrents
Feeling like I'm drowning, will these feelings ever halt?

The fire

I was 16 when you started the fire
Leaving me burnt and exposed
Like a forest after it's been charred
Desolate and barren
Bare of any growth
But even forests start to grow again.

I bore the fruit of 2 precious seeds that grew inside of me… my womb the forest that sprang to life after the fire.

My gifts from mother nature.

Lava

The shame I felt in my soul after your corruption
In my blood, bubbles like hot lava from a volcano
Molten, like after an eruption.

Briars

Wrapping round my aching heart
Branches and thorny briars.
Suffocating, without oxygen
In my soul, dark like waning fires.

False Faces

All you need to do is wear a mask
Paint a picture to the world, not much to ask?.
Put on the false face
Stay in line, know your place.
Wear that smile, look like your shit's together
You seem that strong woman, true emotions to sever.
Under the mask, I am falling apart
From abuse, trauma and a broken heart.
Bury it deep my babe, is what you taught me
Don't have it on display for the world to see.
Always be presentable, no matter the price
Fix your hair, wear nice clothes… no one will know emotions are buried in ice.

Haunted

Once upon a dream
I use to scream
Haunted by the terror within
Visions of past pain and sin.

A little bit of hindsight
for the next 2 poems...

After my mum and dad split up (1996), he went to live back on his family land. He has recently sold this in spring of 2022. To best understand and make sense of some of my deep rooted trauma- which has been intergenerational to a degree- I had to go and revisit where I started the first 4 years of my life.... Our family from his side, has it's fair share of secrets, some better left unsaid and they are not mine to share. Only the land knows...

The darkness in the soil

A darkness sown deep in the soil

Blackness seeps across land, like oil.

What disturbing secrets a place can keep

Full of pain, hurt and turmoil that will make you weep.

Family roots planted firmly over time

Dirty and shameful, some despicable crime.

Memories there that are embedded in the ground

Some buried so deep, they'll never be found.

So it comes for the cursed place to be sold

Someone else can have the trauma of the land, that will now never be told.

Buried

Deep buried fear, secrets, trauma and lies
Rotten land like flesh, being swarmed by flies.
Even when sunny, always a darkness across the skies.
Roots so embedded with the strength of a beating heart
Deceit grows all around, never being picked apart
Brambles and thorns toxic, like a poison dart.
A barren wasteland that to which time has not been kind
Weeds cover the truth that has been hard to find
One last walk there to set fire to the land, leave the past behind.

LESSON TWO

When the unravelling gets messy as F..k

The truth I came to when dealing with years and years of trauma, is it gets messy as fuck. There is no way round this and that one sentence is something we all have to go through if we want to heal. I found myself writing from how I thought I should be perceived, not from how I was actually feeling, being untruthful with myself and my coach.

When you start to unpeel the layers and unravel, it is messy and emotional, experiencing pain you never knew you could. One minute you are up, then down, questioning yourself over and over again, beating yourself up. Feeling guilt, shame, embarrassment, anger, sadness. So many icky nasty feelings, ones that are super hard to wade through, navigate and don't forget tears, lots of tears.

I have always struggled with feeling like a fraud, putting on a mask and painting to the world – I've got this shit – when in fact underneath I was completely falling apart.

Owning my truth has been a huge learning curve for me, having to let go of ego, accept judgements on me and judgements I make

(because even if you think you're not judgey, sorry it's human nature) and the need to paint a picture of myself to the world just to feel worthy and validated. No one needs that kind of pressure on themselves. We live in a world all about appearances, likes, follows etc, also placing expectations on ourselves to conform in a certain way. Such issues are what I struggled with for years and years, since being a young girl. People pleasing, abandonment issues, not feeling worthy enough to have anything good in my life or to experience true happiness and joy.

I have had to try and rewire my whole perception of myself to get into alignment with that. It is not just on a conscious level, it is deep within on a subconscious level, cellular even. I have had to fight my inner child, when she has just needed nurturing, telling her "it is O.K. to be felt, seen, heard and soothed".

Digging deep was never going to be easy and I can assure you it has not been and won't be for you either. It has been one of the hardest, scariest, most uncomfortable things I have ever had to do.

But I am here, stepping out and sharing my story – warts and all – going through the spaghetti junction of string that Is my journey to recovery, truth and authenticity.

Brotherly love

When I started to unravel, I had to examine my relationships with various family members and friends.

Unpicking the role I took on with my brother was an eye opener for me as I didn't acknowledge for a long time, I was trying to be his mum.

I think having had to adopt a mothering role towards him from a young age, I felt responsible to a degree for the path he had walked down.

The mother role with him became a problem as we grew and changed. Our lives took vastly different courses, although looking back now we were just the same messed up kids, becoming traumatised adults.

We both turned to drugs, sought out validation and affection from where ever we could get it. Trying to fill the need for escape and love.

As soon as I started to examine our relationship dynamic, I soon saw I needed to just be his big sister, needless to say our relationship then went from strength to strength.

We listened to each other, making up for lost years we had fighting, letting go of my self-blame and guilt I felt due to both our choices we had made. I felt unduly responsible for him.

We hold a space now for one another and are able to talk things through without judgement or friction arising.

I am so proud of the man he has now become, how much he has grown and changed as a person and I can finally say we have each other's back, just as I always sought it to be.

Total contradiction

I am a total contradiction between dark and light-
I am blind, yet have insight-
I am grounded, yet ready to take flight-
I am placid to the wrong, yet with myself I do fight-
Emotions are like waves, some smooth, some rough-
I have done so much good, yet never feel enough-
My eyes are open, yet I cannot see-
I do not help myself, put others before me-
Why am I like this, my mind starts to wonder-
I can figure others out, but with myself I do ponder-
To others I am generous, warm and kind-
I've been told someone like me is hard to find-
I now need to believe this for peace of mind-
Embracing the new me, leaving the past behind.

Retreat

I am anxious, worried, scared
To many feelings were bared.
I am tired, exhausted worn out
I don't want to share, full of doubt.
I choose self-care, I choose to retreat
Because sometimes the feels are hard to beat.
I am not being selfish, rude or unkind
I need to replenish my soul, spirit and mind.
When I retreat I am still here for you
I still love and care about all that you do.
If I seem distant or so far away
I am doing what I need to just get through the day.

Crab

When I am feeling sad, down and low
Retreat into my shell, like a crab I do go.
A protective armour, my little shell
I hide away here, until I feel well.

Mistress

I am the mistress of masks
What do you mean?, one asks.
Why I have many faces, is what I do mean
Not everyone I have gets to be seen.
The one's you see are of happy, strong me
One who is balanced, together, care free.
Sometimes they slip and I feel ashamed
Showing the sadness inside, that can't be tamed.
I was the mistress of mask, now my faces are true
I've stepped out to show the world, my real self to you.
The faces that are scared, unsure, when feelings are bared
Trauma to truth I have shared.

Inner child

This is one of the first times I have written about this so deeply and been totally honest with myself – it is now April 2021 and I have been on my journey for a year.

My truth is that I am insecure, my little girl inside feel like she needs constant validation and feels rejection easily. Feelings of being ignored, do not sit well inside.

I think it is because as I child I spent a lot of time being ignored and living in fear. I feel annoyed at myself and silly for feeling these emotions. I want to scream out loud "hey notice me" "why are you ignoring me? You're meant to be my guide here!". I am annoyed I still feel needy at times, that I fear rejection still, especially from those that are meant to be there to get you through these darker, difficult periods.

I feel abandoned, but it is not their fault, it's my built up perception of their roles.

My little girl needs constant approval. I need constant approval but I know deep down I have got this. I know I am a strong, resilient, independent woman who has gotten over more than most.

I know I am intelligent and slay at writing poetry, exploring my shadows and showing courage to go there into the darkness.

I can say all these things, so the perception of me is I do have this, that my shit is well and truly together. When actually I feel like a total fraud.

My little girl inside still needs nurturing and telling she is safe, worthy, she is able, she is validated, she is… loved.

I can tell her all these things, but to actually feel them and believe them is a different matter.

However, this is not the woman talking, it's that little girl. The little girl who needs a hug, who needs love but only that can come from me, come from within. I need to let her cry, let her release her pent up emotions instead of squashing them down, just like we are use to. Most importantly though, I need to stop being scared.

Inside, outside

Writings from the child on the inside vs the woman I am on the outside…

The woman on the outside, often scolds the little girl on the inside. Really what the little girl needs is security, reassurance and validation.

There seems to be a constant war between my little girl and my womanly self. The thing is the 2 are the same and both are as valid and intertwined as each other.

Claire

Little Claire I know you are there, you think I don't care but I do
Hiding in the darkest depths me and you.
Little Claire come into the light
My arms of love and safety, hold you tight.
Little Claire I got you, safe and secure
Scared, abandoned, invisible no more.

LESSON THREE

Anger

Anger is one of the emotions I have struggled the most to accept and most importantly feel.

I spent so long not allowing myself to get angry because anger equated to danger in my world. It was always quick to flare in those unsavoury people from the past and the outcome was never a good one.

I associated anger with abuse, so when it came to feeling my own anger and rage, I would just squash it down, not letting it be felt, not wanting to feel like an abuser.

I completely internalised what I was feeling, often directing the anger at myself.

It built inside, like a volcano waiting to erupt after years and years of bring dormant. It came out in self-loathing, victimhood, disassociation from my situation, being distant and holding those involved in total distain and contempt.

I literally ended up hating the party involved and myself for my people pleasing behaviour, perceiving myself as weak for not fighting back or sticking up for myself.

However, it was not safe for me to do any of those things, not safe to show anger, frustration or rage. In hindsight I was not weak, I was in fact showing strength and control in those moments, doing what I had to too stay safe and survive, protecting my children.

st let myself feel the fury and injustice of it all, it was like a torrent of lava flowing. I write and wrote furiously. I allowed all those awful feelings, words and suppression to come out into the light.

I did not know someone could feel so much anger, that it could be kept inside for as long as it had been… I felt vengeful, hateful, which then in turn scared me that I could feel that way.

It made feel what I was trying so hard to escape… being that victim. I felt anger of rejection, anger of putting my life on hold, anger of wasting my love on some guy that did not deserve that privilege and anger at giving my all to those who were not worthy... I however hasten to add it felt so good to rage and let it all out.

Of course, this did pass, it passwd with every trauma I unearthed and spoke about. It passed with every line and word I wrote, like blood spilling onto a page.

I rarely get angry now, not because I am internalising anymore, it's because I don't feel I need to. I mainly feel frustration and annoyance, it is not all out eruption time!

On the occasions I do feel anger or outrage, it is usually because someone has over stepped my boundaries repeatedly, done something that goes against my values or morals and shown disrespectful behaviour towards me or my loved ones. Hell hath no fury like a mumma bear protecting her cubs!

It is ultimately okay to feel this way. As long as your anger is not causing undue harm to anyone else. It is healthy to let it out in a controlled way. To process calmly, giving yourself time to cool down, if you can, before reacting. Finding a healthy outlet for that anger.

Turning it into fuel, power and motivation to implement change and if your me, fight for the ones who cannot fight for themselves.

Revenge

There's a storm brewing, just underneath the surface
Swirling like a hurricane through my veins
Dark and brooding, like thunder clouds over head.

LESSON FOUR

Domestic abuse and predators

My first experience of domestic abuse was when I was 4 years old between my mum and my dad.

This then shaped my behaviour growing up around men and women alike. I was quiet, shy, submissive and living in a constant state of flight, fight, freeze and fawn, only I didn't fight. Mum tried her best to protect my brother and I from the verbal abuse and sometimes weekly violence – she did what she had to do to survive.

As I grew into my teenage years and my dad left, my brother and I bore witness to the damage it had cause our mum – she was finally free after 20 years and couldn't be present as we needed her to be. It resulted in me leaving home, whilst trying to juggle school and bringing up my brother for a time. We were all wounded and suffering the effects of what we had all been through.

I use to blame my mum, but after having my daughter at 21, I healed my mother wound and could see fully the choices she had to make and why. Thankfully we have a strong relationship now and it is where I get my fighting spirit from.

The effects from early childhood abuse and trauma were to be long lasting and a running theme through the years. It shaped my choice in men and I just seemed to attract people, women included, who I let take advantage of me because I had no boundaries, no self- worth.

Starting with being groomed at 16 (as previously mentioned) I had a string of abusive partners - all with differing severity, tactics and behaviours.

The worst 2 by far were my sons father (2008) and the one who raped me in 2010. I was told by my domestic abuse support worker I was lucky to be alive after my sons father. That is a sobering thought. One that made me feel sick to the pit of my stomach and full of shame and guilt as I vowed when I had my daughter, I would never put her through what we went through. It turns out I did the exact opposite and had no conscious idea I was attracting these types of men. They were all charming in the beginning, taking an interest, listening to your sad stories, just so they can reel you in and find your vulnerability.

I have been asked myself and heard so many times "why didn't you just leave" "how did you get yourself into that situation?" – The answers are, until you have been through it, you have no idea how much bravery and courage it takes to leave and secondly, no one goes into a relationship knowing they are going to be abused by that person. They are predators hunting prey. Hindsight (IF you are lucky enough to escape) is a bitch.

I cannot stress enough, sometimes, most of the time, it isn't safe to leave or it's just too terrifying – not knowing the outcome or repercussions if you do go. It is a huge, frightening decision to make, so never minimise or underestimate the enormity of that decision because sometimes there is no choice. Sometimes we are so trauma bonded to that person, we cannot fathom being without them, we love them so much despite the abuse and even after we have left, a trauma bond can remain strong for a long time after.

I met my ex-husband in 2013, confident that this time I chose right.

It took a few months to appear, but he ended up being abusive, but because it was different and not as bad as the others, I couldn't see it. Most of the time he was kind, loving, attentive but there was an undercurrent flowing there, that could drag you under at any time.

It was when it started to affect my children that I made the choice to ask him to leave. That was December 2016 and it is where my healing journey began.

I used my survival story to advocate for other women who had been through similar experiences, to show them that you can go from just surviving to thriving. Sharing my truth, being real and giving a sense of hope and reassurance that we got through the bad and there is good for us, who have been fortunate to get out and most importantly, stay safe, as sadly many women and men do not have that option.

I want to add that not all men are the same, there are great ones out there, such as my step-dad (the man I refer to as dad too) he has shown me support, love, care and guidance for the last 20 years and for that I am eternally grateful.

I have also been able to build a relationship with my dad and that has been largely down to me healing, understanding generational trauma from his side, finding acceptance and mainly finding it in my heart to forgive.

The poems I am going to include here will be dated, as some of them were written after break ups, when I still thought I loved the perpetrator. Some were written as my healing journey began as I started the repairing process and come to terms with the domestic abuse I had been through and likewise witnessed. Also from the experience of my 2 children.

They can be hard hitting but are truthful. They are for the survivors and those who sadly did not survive.

FEB 2019

You're angry, you're sad
You're crazy, you're mad
It's your fault I'm bad.

HE SAID

But I love you, I adore you
I need you to change
I'll love you more, if you stop acting so strange.

HE SAID

O.K I'm sorry, I must be all that you call me
Cause you love me and that I can see
Even though myself, I cannot be?

SHE SAID

You're frigid, there's no affection
You must be cheating
Come here now, show me love, despite the beating
Or I'm leaving.

HE SAID

What can I do to make you stay?
To treat me better, keep the bruises at bay?
Let's go to bed…

SHE SAID

You're lucky I haven't killed you
I hate everything you do
You're a useless waste of space
Just fuck off out of my face.

HE SAID

It's O.K I will try harder to please
I will cry and beg, be down on my knees
I can be a good partner, just show me how
Although the damage is done to me now.

SHE SAID

You're disgusting, disgraceful
A shame to human kind
You've really done it now
You are out of your mind
Scum like you should be behind bars
You have definitely taken it to far.

THE POLICEMAN SAID

"I'm going to leave" were her final words
But now those words, won't be heard
As we are met by a vow of silence
From this awful act of domestic violence
There is nothing left at all
This was to be her final fall.

SHE'S DEAD….

Feb 2019

Tummy Ache

Mummy I have a tummy ache
I get it when the shouting starts and I begin to shake.
Mummy I don't want to go to school and leave you at home
I am scared of what will happen, when I leave you on your own.
Mummy I have a tummy ache, I get butterflies inside
I saw the bruises on your face, you said you fell, I knew you lied.
I know you try your best to hide, that he causes hurt to you
Mummy when will these men stop hurting you like they do?
Mummy I get nightmares, I'm scared to go to sleep
Because when I try to stay in bed, I can hear you cry and weep.
Mummy I lay in bed at night and listen to you fight
I curl up in a ball and hold my teddy so tight.
Mummy I never see you smile, I only see you sad
I wonder if it's something I've done, does he hurt you cause I'm bad?
He always shouts and calls us names, he is always mad.

Sometimes when you're arguing, I stand there crying
I get so frightened on my own, hearing voices flying.
Then one day we had to leave, I was confused why we had to go
But then the policeman came, my bruises I had to show.
Now that HE has gone and mum it is just us
I can start to feel safe and again begin to trust.
Mummy as the months have gone by and we are happy on our own
The butterflies and my tummy aches have gone, my trust in others has grown.
Mummy we are now a happy family and I dream nice dreams at night
The one thing that I love the most is you tucking me in and hugging me tight.
Mummy I love you so much and I know how much you care
Because mum it us just us and at last you're always there.

Voiceless

I feel voiceless, in a world swirling with words
I feel voiceless, my words can't be heard.
Speaking my truth is all I want to do
But my voice is to small, not loud like you.
I feel voiceless, I was always told to hush
I feel voiceless, no time to talk, always a rush.
I feel voiceless, your words, my soul they do shatter
I feel voiceless, after all my voice doesn't matter.

SOMETIME NEAR THE MIDDLE OF 2011

Weather pain

As tears fall from my eyes, like the sky full of rain
I wonder if they'll wash away my pain?.
For you were the sunlight that first brightened up my day
Then the dark clouds came and the sun shied away.
Feelings of lust, like lightning in my veins
The imminent thunder took them away again.
A whirlwind of emotions, through our relationship blew
The stormiest times became more frequent, grew.
The sunbeams broke through with a glimmer of light
Darkness came calling to put up a fight
The rain fell again, sun out of sight.
With a crash and a bang, a crackle and a flash
The sun tried to break through, give it one more bash.
Through the mixture of emotions a rainbow did appear
To make the sunbeam and the rain, see there's nothing to fear.
Our lives like the weather, may change from day to day
But the sun saw off the rain and the brightness did stay.

SUMMER **2011**

realisation

All the things you've put me through, has torn my soul apart
So why do I feel like there's a black hole, deep in my heart?.
You don't deserve my bitterness, sadness and tears
Because you abused what love I gave you and played upon my fears.
You loved me like no other- that is what you said
So how could you cheat? And take another to bed?.
Maybe you did- who knows what ran round your head?
Did you just keep me sweet, as your addiction I fed?.
I felt from you love, like I'd never been shown
What was to happen, was at the time, not known
By the time it happened, it was too late, feelings had grown
What you did to me, self-dignity, respect, out the window was thrown.
All the cheating pain, hurt and deceit
When you did what you did, my heart no longer wanted to beat.
You used my body without consent or respect
You weren't meant to do that, you said you'd love and protect.
An animal that night to fulfil your own pleasure

The humiliation, pain and anguish in me – no one could measure.
You took what was mine and used it for you
Even when I told you STOP, you carried on, was nothing I could do.
Helpless and scared from your predatory attack
I cannot believe this was happening again- why did I take you back?
When I cried out in pain, you said "you'd be done in a while"
For those minutes you carried on, I felt so vile.
After you had finished, I sat there with tears streaming from my eyes
You said not to tell, no one would believe me, they'd think it all lies.
You showed no remorse or said no apology, for what you had just done
You just wondered why I didn't see it as just a "little fun".
The look in your eyes was one I had seen many times before
I should have seen sense and booted you out the door.
Heavily influenced by the drugs you had taken
You were wrecked, I was far from mistaken.
That was something to hide behind for you- your drug misuse
But what you had just done, there was no damned excuse.
As I'm sat here writing this, I don't feel angry or mad
Because for you, I don't know why, I feel very sad.
My life I can slowly start to rebuild and repair
You on the other hand, life is full of guilt, shame and despair.
I hope one day you'll get the help, you so need
And your head no longer fuel the habit that you feed.
I hope one day you'll realise all the pain that you've dished out
If not you'll keep on preying on the innocent, I have no doubt…..

June 2020 — 2022

Mud

Not all men are the same…
"aren't they?" said the muddied heart.
There are good men out there- the question reframed
"are there?" replied the muddied heart- again…

Invasion

I feel invaded, like a once untouched paradise
Now ravaged and destroyed by too many men treading there.

1)

You might deny you forcefully took from my body, which I did not want to give…
But at least I can sleep at night.

2)

I will not let you steal my dreams.. as you created my nightmares.

3)

Vomiting red, hurt pain and dread
Spewing black, toxicity where demons tread.
Shadows drawn from words unsaid
The colours of torment, in my head.

LESSON FIVE

Combating the F word

It makes sense that this should come next for you, the reader as I take you through my journey.

Fear is what has held me back from writing this sooner. It has been the crippling fear of failure. It Is true, failing is after all learning and we all need to make mistakes in life, to fail, to learn. There is a great difference between the word fail and the word mistake though. Fail is much more of a definitive word. So put it along with fear, is why many of us, do not put ourselves out there and refuse to be seen. We don't follow our dreams, do not go for what we truly desire or would like in our lives.

Growing up, never being recognised for my achievements, being told you're never good enough or you should do this, should do that, impacts greatly from where certain fears come from. For me it is fear of inadequacy and being seen.

We are not born with fear, yet it becomes a part of our lives from a pretty young age.

Being taught fear of hurting yourself, is repeated time and time again as a child. It is designed to keep us "safe", for example:

Don't touch the oven, it will burn you. Stay away from the road, it is dangerous, never talk to strangers….

These are more cautionary warnings, so what happens when fear is used as a damaging, inappropriate action? We all learn to fear specific situations learned through others.

Even in Folklore, fairy tales and myths, fear is used, for example:

"The poison apple" "The dangerous Dragon" "The haunted house".

Fear of spiders, snakes, heights, fire, drowning…the bogey man.

Fear can be healthy to keep us safe but also it can be debilitating, toxic and govern our very existence. It can be crippling – especially when it is fear of those around you, of those that are meant to protect you, those who you love and are supposed to love you back.

A constant state of fight or flight, being so afraid of everything, of everyone, you can no longer trust yourself of what is classed as SAFE, HEALTHY, RIGHT or WRONG.

Growing up in a household where fear is "normal" is not an ideal way to start life. Unsure and not knowing what is going to come next, living in an unpredictable environment, treading on eggshells.

All these feelings caused by a parent, care giver even a family friend. People who are meant to love, nurture and protect you, can cause irreparable damage. Alternatively it can cause lack of fear, making you want to thrill seek, as you have been running on adrenaline your whole life (fight, flight, freeze). The world we create for ourselves can become dysfunctional, seeking out dangerous, unhealthy situations because you can't function without that feeling of being on high alert. Believing you deserve no better than to live in fear, often resulting in fearing yourself, your own mind and own being.

The world seems to run on fear.. the fear of the unknown, the state of the world ,global warming, illness, child abuse, trafficking, rape, corruption and greed… the list goes on.

Fear of moving on, of believing in yourself.

Having to relearn fear can be overcome. You can face it, deal with it, learn to manage it. Not let it consume you.

Be excited about the unknown, embrace what you can achieve, learn the signs to look out for in dangerous people, places. Step out, allow yourself to be seen, be heard. Turn FEAR into COURAGE- YOU'VE GOT THIS BRAVE ONE ….

We are all going to make mistakes, it is how we look at those mistakes and perceive failure.

Shame, guilt, embarrassment – NO

Learning, embracing, courage – YES

Thorns

Insecurities creeping in like thorny vines,

Spreading, growing, suffocating

Drowning in a sea, being caught in a rip tide.

Overwhelmed, anxious, panicking

Heart beats fast, a drum banging.

It is loud in my head

I keep the voices well fed.

Chatter, infiltrating like weeds

So many words, each poison seeds

Hush! Silence is golden indeed.

We all get moments of that constant chatter in our heads. I think making time for it is important, but not to let it take over. Repetitive thoughts, especially when you suffer anxiety, depression, O.C.D and other mental health issues can become crippling.

It is up to us to try, if we can, to work through it gain insight and find healthy coping mechanisms. Thankfully my chatter is less these days. Writing is a huge help for me to release such thoughts, this is my coping mechanism.

My trusted friend

Fear said
Come here my dear
Let me whisper a song in your ear.
So seductive is the voice
She makes you think listening is your choice.
Fear my trusted friend
The one on who I can depend
Until one day the friendship ends.

Sinister lullabies

Like a boogey man waiting to pounce from the shadows
Black, clawed hands, your fears he knows.
The panic that rises, as you fight not to close your eyes
He is whispering in your ears, sinister lullabies.
Finally succumbing to a restless sleep
In his domain, he enjoys hearing you weep.

The mouse

Shying away, shrivelling like a wilted bloom
A fly caught in a web, unaware of impending doom.
The timid mouse, hiding in her hole
The terror felt deep down in my soul.
Panic rising, blood rushing in my ears
Frightened and hiding away from the fears.

Marry me

When fear gets down on a bended knee
"Please will you marry me?"
Yes – I'll take you by the hand
Keep you trapped by the wedding band.
To have and to hold
To cripple and fold
I'll make you mine, until we are grey and old.

Alice

Falling, tumbling, continuing to roll
Just as Alice down the rabbit hole.
Can't find my bearings and come to a halt
Head voices telling me, "it's all your fault".
Back and forth, to and fro
Being lost, overwhelm does grow.
The maze in my mind, is there any way out?
Looking this way and that, feeling horror and doubt.
"You're late, you're late" the white rabbit chatters
"Late for what?" as my voice shatters….

The hole

I am stood silently, looking down a hole
Do I jump, do I roll?
Fall into the darkness, there is no sight
Pitch black, in the dead of night.
Swirling, tumbling
Floundering, fumbling.
Finding a hold, grip on tight
Oh look – here comes the light.

Cheshire cat

When fear is grinning at you like a Cheshire cat
Smile sweetly back – that's not where I'm at.

LESSON SIX

Recovery

This is by far the most detailed part of my journey. I have as of September 2022 been in recovery from drug addiction for 14 years.

I had never given myself credit for that until I started on my healing journey. As you will see though, there have been many layers to unpick and ways in which I have written about addiction, the different types I experienced and how I realised, I was addicted to prescription meds instead. I have lost many close ones to addiction and felt it was so important to include this chapter. I want to start with the poem that means the most to me in my recovery and the very two reasons I chose to remain clean and sober.. my reasons for living… my babies.

My saviour, my gift

I carried you both as seeds in my womb
Where sadly I thought nothing would bloom.
Mother nature had other ideas
I was blessed with you both within years.
My babies sent from the universe above
I grew you both with so much love.
Your souls passed to me, for me to treasure
There is no gift in the world that could ever measure.
When you finally arrived, I felt love like I'd never known
I vowed to protect you always, even when you are grown.
One with eyes of blue, like the ocean, one with eyes green as spring
I wonder what joys to you both life will bring?
Grace my saviour, my starry eyed surprise
Kasen my gift, a miracle in disguise.
I cannot describe how proud of you both I am
I'll shout it from the rooftops, I don't give a damn.
Both so unique and special in your own ways
I will love you my babies, until the end of my days.

The beginning

My addictions started at a very young age, with cleanliness and collecting. It was more of a coping strategy, I have discovered that now. Growing up in an abusive household, I had an addiction to people pleasing- anything to squash confrontation and turmoil.

As I hit my teens I started drinking, as we all did back then, down the park on a Friday and Saturday night, being bought alcohol by strange adults that should have known better.

As documented further down in more detail, my first drug of choice was speed at aged 15. I was never really interested in smoking pot or weed. It was mainly pot back then anyway.

Dirty, dirty speed/base but it gave me an escape, a release from my ever growing, turbulent reality. It gave me confidence and a way to be expressive, it gave me a voice of which before I was to scared to use. It made me feel part of something, less shy and embarrassed about myself.

The adults around us, who should have been protecting us and telling us not to do drugs, including my mum, were all doing it with us.

 It became part of daily life. It was "normal", only it wasn't was it?

Life with a heroin addict…

Seeing people gauging out, eyes rolling, over doses, dirty needles, lies, deception…DISEASE. That is what addiction ultimately is . it eats away at your very being, your soul, your morals.

There is so much I wouldn't change though. I met my still best friend of 25 years, my cheer leader, Miss Sellers.

There was so much I learned, the many lessons it taught me, of course I didn't see that at the time but reflecting back now, I can.

I had some of the best times, connecting with the people I treasured most in this world and still do, even though some of them are gone. Succumbed to their own addictions and personal hell. I thank you though Mumma T for the love you showed me through everything, through the chaos, for giving us waifs and strays a home, for loving us despite all your demons you had to fight…. I miss you babe.

The first step in rescuing myself was to realise no amount of drugs will help you hide forever, if anything in the end it amplifies the pain, shame and fear. I had to find my self-worth, stop rescuing others, who in turn abused me like a drug, I became addicted to rescuing them though. It was a hard habit to break but I did it and now I am free and freedom is what I was lucky enough to find. I will never take that for granted though and live each day as it comes.

Dancing with the devil

My affair with drugs first started when I was introduced to speed aged 15. I soon progressed to ecstasy and Valium to come down. Everyone in the late 90s were at it. Plus I had a 29 year old boyfriend, who was a recovering heroin addict. Recovering until I found him slumped up against a cupboard with works hanging out of his arm. One of many o.ds I'd witness in a year. This man also introduced many of the lads I hung around with, to the brown ways. It was unforgiveable the destruction it later caused for their lives, some even losing their lives.

I then found the white stuff at 18.. oh cocaine, where a gram would last 2 of you most of the night. Then there was the grab bag – a mixture of all types of prescription tranquillizers – Valium, Temazepam, Nitrazepam, Librium, DF118S…. such a hazy concoction. We used to joke I never started on class C, I went straight to class A.

After becoming clean when I had my daughter at 21, I was on the wagon for 4 years, I fell off again for 18 months with the white stuff and Valium. I then fell pregnant with my baby boy.

This was a turning point for me and I became clean and sober, September 2008…. Or so I thought.

I worked so hard to get clean from illegal drugs, I didn't see I had formed an entirely new addiction altogether. No one warns you about the addiction to legal prescription drugs.

I had suffered for many years with chronic pain. I had varying gynaecological issues, I had damaged a nerve in my back. I eventually got diagnosed with Fibromyalgia and Degenerative Arthritis in 2005 when Fibro was still relatively unheard of.

For years I took codeine to manage pain, but that's not addictive… right?

Fast forward to 2009, when I had a 5 month old baby and needed a hysterectomy. They gave me morphine and Oramorph to come home with. I thought I was in control and sure I stopped the Oramorph but was still living on Codeine . taking up to 180mg a day.

June 2010 is when the shit hit the fan. I had to go in for major hip surgery. This is when my Morphine dependency started. No one tells you how easy it is to get hooked, I believe this is why there is a huge worldwide Opioid epidemic.

I had complications from the surgery so I was given slow release Morphine capsules called Zomorph. I started with 10mg in the morning and 20mg at night. I was soon up to 30mg in the morning and 60mg at night, with Oramorph on top and Amitriptyline (which made me feel suicidal) I wondered how the hell I was still functioning at this point?. I was though and use to joke how I was a legal heroin addict and oh how the weight of that hit me when my then boyfriend started stealing my meds to aid his hidden heroin addiction. I can honestly hand on heart say, I would never have gone down that route as I watched it destroy so many lives.

However I battled for many years in my mind, regardless that it was legal, I was an opioid addict.. pure and simple.

In early 2013 I met my ex -husband and I decided I was going to wean myself off my tablets. I managed over time to get down from 120mg a day of Zomorph to the 60mg a day, plus I was taking 30mg of Mirtazapine for depression and anxiety.

 I still needed to do better, but I was managing and it was enough to take the edge off the pain and still function, so that is where I stayed.

My ex-husband and I split in December 2016, then in January 2017 my dad had a heart attack and then my nan died unexpectedly, it is safe to say I was not coping at this point. The doctor out me on Zopiclone, a very strong sedative but it didn't work. I knew, I could see, I just wanted to take anything to numb the pain. I wanted to make it go away, but to everyone else I showed I was doing fine on the outside- yes that good old mask! – whereas inside I was breaking and being self-destructive with my thoughts.

I told the doctor to not let me have those again, but he did… didn't even question it when I asked again. I did ask to come off the Zomorph but due to many other deaths over the next 2 years, anxiety and stress, I was left on them .

This takes us to 2019… I hadn't had any med review for years and a routine blood test showed my kidney function was low and the cause was Zomorph. I spoke to a new doctor and he was horrified I and been on Zomorph as long as I had been (10 years) and taking them alongside Pregabalin and Mirtazapine, so he suggested doing a controlled drop… lets go for it I said… this was Jan 2020.

Slowly a 10mg drop every 3 weeks, that should be easy, right? I am only on 30mg twice a day.

I bossed the first drop 20mg/30mg

The second 20mg/20mg

The third 10mg/20mg

Replacing it with 150mg of pregabalin a day… then came hell…

Shaking, shivering, stomach cramps, I couldn't move, get out of bed. I couldn't stop crying and wanted to tear my skin off, the itching was un-bearable, feeling like my skin was crawling. I was waking up every hour, anxiety through the roof. I even had to call an ambulance at one point just as covid hit, the crew thought I had covid I was that unwell but it turns out I was in withdrawal and having a reaction to Pregabalin. This continued for 10 days… then just like the sun coming out in the spring, I was okay…

I was off Pregabalin, clean off Morphine and I could manage my pain myself, in fact my pain was much better. I felt the best I had in a decade but I also put this down to dealing with my trauma and it being released from my body. I thank that doctor for a fresh pair of eyes.

I now take 150mg of Pregabalin at night as this is when my pain is worst and 45mg of Mirtazapine as it stabilises my mood.

Big pharma has a lot to answer for, they need to be held accountable for the epidemic sweeping the world. This has been a real eye opener for me and a journey to at long last, clarity.

The Brown Lady who calls

You came into my life, I knew just what you were
But even though I knew it, my feelings did not deter.
At first it was okay and somehow I did cope
The brown lady kept on calling, there was no hope.
Manic, loving, hyper, was your general mood
And from your skin and body, sweat did pour, exude.
Then came the rattle and she was clutching at your veins
Sickness, cramping, illness, was her revenge to cause you pain.
This brown lady is a weakness, one riddled with disease
And even though you tried to resist her, her whisper made you weak at the knees.
She whispered soft, then shouted loud
"come back to me baby, you'll make me so proud".
So creeping off, like a man, who is hiding an affair
The brown lady reeled you in, trapped you deep in her snare.
For when you've left that bitch, your weakness she will find
Causing doubts and bad feelings deep in your mind.
She makes you lose once again the happiness you have found
So here you are again, to the brown lady you are bound.

Rotten Delicious

Despite the poison apple looking delicious, we all know it was rotten to the core and delivered a nasty surprise to dear Snow White.

Only in this tale there was no prince to come and wake this princess, oh no no, the only one waking this Princess was herself.

Let's start at the beginning of this tale of self- heroism.

As previously mentioned, my earliest memory was that of violence, aged just 4 witnessing my dad's hands round my mums throat… what an environment to be growing up in. Fight, flight, shyness, anxiety, learning to tread on eggshells. As long as I was seen and not heard, only when it was allowed, I was safe.

It was not just at home, it was school too. The shy, quiet little blonde girl who was unassuming, who got bullied relentlessly for being that way, too scared to speak out. I felt exposed, voiceless and just wanted to be invisible. The more I tried to be invisible, the worse it became. I was belittled and ridiculed by teachers as I didn't participate enough in class or if I did I went as scarlet as Snow White's apple.

Fast forward to 15… we know what happened here as it has been previously mentioned. Dad had left, mum off the rails after finding her freedom. Me playing mum to my brother, bunking school, then the rotten delicious came along.

The toxicity becomes delicious until you want to crave more and more, taking bigger bites out of that big red juicy apple. You become addicted to the rush of the sweetness of said apple.

I refer to this part as rotten delicious, because when you know no difference, that big red shiny apple is so appealing, so alluring… so … delicious.

Being rotten myself inside, addicted … addicted to that poison, that toxicity, myself becoming poisoned, becoming rotten, whilst all the while trying to remain delicious.

I was Snow Whites apple, I was the Witch that poisoned me… I then chose to keep eating and poison myself, taking bigger and bigger bites.

It didn't matter anymore… I was rotten to my core.

The Gnome

It is very safe to say, I met some pretty unsavoury characters during my drug addiction.

I never felt the need to write about them really, but it came to me one day that this particular character, who shall be referred to as the gnome, was a integral part to not just mine, but others drug addiction too. It was pretty icky having to dig deep with this one as I had blocked so much of it out, not wanting to face up to the shame I felt for having gotten myself in some less than desirable predicaments… but if I want to heal, I have to go to the deepest, darkest caverns in my subconscious and bring what lives there out into the light.

So the gnome supplied us all with drugs, mainly us young women at the time and often for free, under the ruse of friendship. I had no reliant father figure at the time, so think maybe I was searching for that? I wasn't the only one, he preyed on us all. In hindsight, reflecting, it must have given him some warped power trip.

Don't get me wrong, I can't speak for the others and neither would I want to, but I know myself I took advantage of him too.

I wasn't blameless and my moral compass was very much broken. I was in the height of my addiction.

Looking back, it makes me feel sick to the pit of my stomach, repulsed, really strong words I know but true. When I think of him it gives me the creeps and can see how toxic and dysfunctional the whole dynamic was.

The guy was a dealer, he dished out the drugs to stroke his ego. The reality was, he was a sad, lonely old man- but was anything but lonely- but was he deep down.

He must have known we were using him as much as he was using us? Drugs on tap, party central and really who wouldn't take free drugs? However they weren't really free were they? It cost me my pride, my dignity and most of all myself… it taught me that actually nothing in this world is free, all vices have a price.

Just one more

Just one more line
Go on you'll be fine.
Just one more gram
Okay, I don't give a damn.
Just one more line
I'm not feeling fine
Don't be silly, it'd all in your mind.
Not one more gram
Oh now you give a damn
A damn to how I am…

White

1)

As pristine as newly laid snow, powdered and white
The snow keeps on falling deep into the night.
Wake up in the morning and it's all turned to slush
Foggy and groggy, soft like mush.

2)

The snow keeps on falling here all year round
It's getting so deep, you can't see the ground.
I need digging out, to feel safe and sound
Warm in the comfort of clean, I have now found.

The mountain

Recovery is like climbing a mountain but when you reach the top and see that beautiful, clear view, the effort was worth it.

Recovery is a dark place

Dealing with shame and guilt is hard to face

Recovery is a challenge, a slow pace.

Recovery is freedom from hazy days

Recovery I'll be in always.

Recovery is strength like you've never known

Be proud of the courage that you have shown.

The road to recovery is not easy, it is tough. It is painful. It is messy. I struggled with shame and guilt the most, it took me to some really dark places, places I did not want to go.

So many questions of why did I do that? How could I do that? Did I really do that?.

These "that's" I am referring to are the many situations I found myself in. Spending all my wages(before I had kids) in 3 nights, sleeping with men I never would have, had I been clean and sober, walking late at night when I was high, by myself.

Getting up and being fed speed for breakfast when I was 16, taking ecstasy tablets so I would perform and being used as a sex toy. Hanging out with dealers. Spending money I shouldn't have when I had my daughter, taking out loans left, right and centre. Having people in my home that should not have been there, my daughter seeing fights between me and my then partner. It was chaotic. It sounds awful doesn't it?

Not everyone's experience is like this though, it is very personal, depending on the drug of choice. I have shared this to show you that you are not alone in how you might be feeling or have felt. I have detailed hugely personal experiences, being authentic is an extremely important part of my continued recovery.

Recovery is hard… but the truth, at the end, when you have got through the mud, the storm, the darkness, is magnificent.

To feel free, to accomplish something so personal, to feel lighter. Recovery is life long, It is a road we have to walk continually but it gets easier as the years go by.

It has for me and I feel proud each time I hit a milestone. Recovery is part of me, it always will be.

Recovery most importantly has become my friend, my companion and I embrace and cherish that friendship every day.

It might not be tips on how to get clean or sober as everyone has their own path, I just hope this can help you feel less alone than I did.

Resides

Dancing with Demons
The Angel doesn't always win
The Demon raises her beautifully ugly but oh so necessary head
She roars and screams to be heard, to be felt, to be free
I tame her, dance with her, let her stay
Only on my terms does she still reside in me
I don't want to be free of her, she has served me well.
The Angel comforts her and they become friends
After all light and dark lives within us all.

LESSON SEVEN

Grief, love and loss

To get to where I need to be, I have had to- albeit not very well I hasten to add- the overwhelming loss I have experienced over my adult life, mainly the last 13 years, most of which I haven't dealt with and thought I had, but writing this chapter, It is clear I have not.

I am not talking just death, although I can assure you there has been far to man to count, but of love, friendship and loss of myself.

I have found it does not matter how toxic a relationship of any kind was, it still hurts, sometimes even more so when it ends. Especially if it is a relationship where you have been controlled or abused.

I have loved in many ways, I have lost in many ways but I have chosen (apart from when the dear but shitty father death has come calling) to create loss for myself, as I know those relationships were making me lose myself and were bad for my over- all health.

Watching my Nanna and my Auntie die in front of me, fundamentally changed me.

At the same time I felt honoured to be there to share those last moments with them, to watch them take their last breath, t watch their pain and suffering be no more.

I believe that my spiritual journey and belief in the after life has helped me when I have lost a loved one to death. I know their soul has just moved on to the next stage of their journey in this world.

Grief has been sitting as a lump in my chest, festering away, not realising the hardened wall I have built up. I have not felt whole in some time. I have felt broken and numb.

I am scared to start attempting to take down the wall, it feels like a dam cracking and I am fearful of the torrent that is waiting to burst out, not being able to swim and drowning in deep emotion, being dragged down to the murky depths.

I have survived the flood before, I am a strong swimmer and know I will stay afloat in the ever changing current that is grief and loss.

Submerge

Submerged in a rip tide of emotion
Head held down, swept away to deep ocean.
Fighting against the current, dragged down to the abyss
The abyss where happiness is amiss.

Grey of the day

When the colour gets sucked away, everything is grey
A vastness of grey on a cloudy day.
The colours kept at bay.
Sadness is the only colour I can see
The grey of the cloud that lives in me.

Stones

I have collected many stones over my life, mainly the last 8 years
The stones I have collected weighed me down and brought many tears.
Tears have stopped coming, stones built up a wall
A wall where there is now no feeling at all.
The feelings worn away like stones into sand
Sand slips away when in the palm of your hand.
In my hand I could never hold the weight of my sadness
Stones of sadness and grief, no order, just mess.
The heaviness of the stones I hold in my heart, on my shoulders
My shoulders and heart aches, the grief like boulders.
Boulders and stones that eventually erode away
Away they erode, but fragments will stay.

FRAGMENTS

I am fragmented, my broken heart in tiny shards of loss, being held together with delicate spun glass that could shatter at any given moment.

I sometimes wonder how I have held myself together for so long, unable to feel, building up walls, masking my sadness and going through the motions.

Fragments of myself being lost with each loved one taken, each relationship that ends, each trauma that happens, the loss of myself.

I will pick up the pieces and rebuild myself through my grief, I will acknowledge as I have done many times before my loss and slowly the fragments will come back as a whole. My heart will mend and I will be able to love and be loved as I deserve to be.

Pieces of you

Fragments of memories I try to piece together of you
I can picture you so clearly, you with the eyes so blue.
I wish I could forget, my heart has an ache
You were the best and the worst, my favourite mistake.

Drifting

1)

When I drift, I drift to you
To you I drift with eyes so blue.
I drift to a life that could have been
A life only my dreams have seen.
My dreams that always drift to you
Drift to you with the eyes so blue.

2)

You left me with so many words left to say
You left for good, not to come back another day.
I am drifting with a heart that's been broken
Broken from words unspoken.
Spoken to you for you to hear
Hear in my heart I held you so dear.

The bear

1)

Tethered together by centuries of lives past
An illicit love affair that was never going to last.
I use to dream of what could have been
What did loosing you twice this lifetime mean?
A connection severed forever?

2)

I grieved you three times in all
This life, once you meant everything, once meant nothing at all.
Did I grieve for what we had all those centuries ago- yes
Did I grieve for who you are now? No I confess.

Nanny

Death is a journey we all expect
But when It decides to take you, it's still hard to accept.
Death is a word, not a kind word too
We can't describe the pain of losing you.
You stayed strong until your very last breath
We were right beside you until you left.
Holding your hand but not back the tears
Memories flew past of all of the years.
Memories of you, we will always treasure
The pain of losing you, no one could measure.
Beauty and dignity are words that remind me of you
No matter the situation you're strength always shone through.
Made up, well presented no matter the time
Even now in death, your beauty still shines.
To see your face or to hear your voice
Wise words that were spoken are gone with no choice.
There are many words left to be spoken
You going to soon has left us all broken.
You have been called up to Heaven above
Gaining your Angel wings, given with love.
I hope that you know, when looking down from up there
You can see how we miss you, love and care.
You weren't just our Nan, you were our friend too
And Nan our dear friend, we will forever miss you.

Twilight dimmed

I watch as the twilight fades from your eyes and your body succumbs to the night.

Knowing your soul will travel to the light of an infinite dawn

Seeing the brightness of the day free from pain.

Peonies

When something beautiful reminds you of a time of great pain. A Peony in bloom, reminds me of you, my Nan. It was your favourite flower. Alas you are no longer here on this Earth plain, you are in a garden full of Peonies, helping them grow and bloom.

So I smile and thank the Peonies with their beautiful blooms, that they remind me of a beautiful woman just as they are, just as you were.

Poppet

Well Auntie Lyn where do I start
Other than the massive hole you have left in our hearts.
You were so beautiful with high cheekbones and big hair
You looked like a young Joan Collins, people would admire and stare.
So vibrant and full of life, what others thought you didn't care
How loved you were and still are, you just weren't aware.
You loved being outside, a gardening ace
So proud of your plants, they put a smile on your face.
You were one of a kind with your lop sided smirks
Your interests and ideas, your little quirks.
Nicknames you had for us all, kiddo, kiddlewinks and poppet
Making me laugh on the phone, shouting at the cats to behave and stop it!.

There is no denying the love you had for your babies- your cats

The way you hid messy hair with one of your many baseball hats.

Even though he did annoy you, you loved your Mart

Shouting, calling him names- you grumpy old fart.

Your dream man George Michael "He's beautiful, but he's gay- what a waste" you did say

We gotta agree, at least you had taste- loved how you worded things in your own way.

Your last few months were filled with sadness and gloom

Now we hope your Heavenly garden is now in full bloom

The last year was tough and it wasn't your best

But good memories we have, so lets put you to rest.

We hate to think you've gone but know you're walking on Gambia's shores

Our lives won't be the same, we will miss you and love you forever more.

Love you always Poppet xxx

Moonshine

My dearest Traze we can't believe you've departed
Your sudden leaving this world, has left us broken hearted.
As your journey will continue on the other side
Your soul and spirit will be on a new ride.
You were one in a million so caring and kind
Someone like you, impossible to find.
With you're knowledge and guidance to me you did show
It helped me so much to develop, change and grow.
With a heart so big and full of light
I know you'll be watching from above, out into the night.
I am your sunbeam, full of sunbeam smiles
You are my moonshine, who's beams shine for miles.
This is not farewell as your essence is still here
Your spirit all around, you'll always be near.
We will hold you in our hearts, this isn't goodbye
All we need to do to see you is look up to the stars in the sky.
We will never forget you the Traze we love and adore
Your light will keep shining on forever more.

Traze was my spiritual mentor and without her, I would not have gotten as far in my spiritual journey as I did. I am forever thankful for her wisdom, courage and belief.

Mumma T

Even though our time together was crazy, insane
We shared the brightest sunshine, the heaviest rain.
You gave me a home, taught me how to be myself
Showed me love and kindness when there was no one else.
So I give thanks to you Mumma T
For showing me how to be.
Always there with open arms and a smile
Now you rest well as it's been a while.
As we stand here to say our goodbyes
You'll be looking at us, vodka in hand, looking down from the skies.
No use trying to keep the tears at bay
Cause babe, Heaven has gained another Angel today.

Teri was my surrogate mum for all intense and purposes. She mothered everyone.

We were a mish mash of misfits, who all accepted each other for who we were. Her kids like brothers and sisters. It was not always a bed of roses, but as the tribute outlines, she took me in and showed me it was okay to be me and I will forever be grateful for her nurturing when I needed it the most.

Rich

I met you when I was just fifteen
You were drunk, language obscene.
But I warmed to you straight away
Until you were taken, in my life you did stay.
Now you're gone, life without you isn't the same
As such a big part of my life you became.
So many memories, some bad and some good
To be here with us now, yes you should.
The smiles, the pain, laughter and tears
We've shared them all over the years.
But no grudges or bad feelings were held onto
No harm was meant, cause you were just you.
I know you loved my mum in your own way
And tried your best every day.
Always forgiven for the things that you did
Sat there sulking like a little kid.
These were the traits we loved and adored
I hope you are at peace, walking on Heavens shores.
Because in Heaven, that is where you are
In my heart and thoughts, you are never far.
I miss you Rich, I'm sure that you know
In my heart you will stay, never away will you go.

Weathered

Curly hair and a weathered face
The pub and beer garden were your favourite place.
You were so proud you came from the south
Can of larger in hand, fag hanging out your mouth.
Baggy tees, checked shorts and trainers were your style
But your mouth use to make some people run a mile!.
All harmless banter did come out
Your friends knew what you were about.
INA KLINA ON THE DICKY DINA
What a catchphrase, no one has had finer!.
But you were suddenly taken from us all
No one could predict your call to Heavens door.
Somehow why you got taken didn't make sense
The people who came to say goodbye were immense.
We loved you Rich and still do
As Rich you were one of a kind, that much was true.

Loss of myself

Aloneness

Standing of a desolate tundra
I look around, there's no one to see.
Just one lonesome tree, that tree is me…
I am frozen, no smile on my face
Roots un-growing, stuck in place.
Cold wind rushing
Aloneness crushing.

Wondering

The space where my life force lies
Shattered shards, my soul cries.
Where have you gone? Were you ever really here?
I am lost you see, I answer, full of fear.
Lost and wondering
Scared and pondering.
Adrift in the void that's my mind
Searching for myself to find.

My truth on making questionable choices

I wrote this back in summer 2020 whilst I was well into my healing journey, examining different relationships and situations I had experienced.

I always thought advice from others came from a place of love and friendship, I came to realise that wasn't always the case.

This all came to me on a beautiful summers day, which was quite poignant as I could feel the sunshine rising in myself.

It is true, I have made many questionable choices in my life.

Although I am my own person and have a valuable, insightful mind of my own, I have often doubted my capability in decision making. In my growth, it has shown me the deep rooted reasons of why I made certain, unhelpful decisions. It boils down to SELF-LOVE, SELF-WORTH, SELF-CONFIDENCE and SELF-TRUST.

I was surrounded by likeminded people, who I believed at the time had my best interests at heart.

As I have worked through my perceptions and beliefs I had about myself, I realised these people did not!.

They wanted me on the same level as themselves.

I was allowing them to advise me on my life, by their standards, on what they would do in my situation. Where I perceived myself to be weak and based on m y trauma led, poor decision making in the past, I thought I was unable to make my own informed and sound choices.

I did not have trust in myself ad valued their advice and solutions over my own. I held them in higher esteem then I did my own mind.

I started to feel and see that they just wanted to keep me at their level, because if I started to raise my esteem then they knew I wouldn't have them in my life any longer. That I would start to see through them and that is what I did. These people were not bad people, they were just as lost I was at the time. These people are no longer in my life anymore.

As I started to grow and change and I started to gain a better understanding of myself, they were no longer happy for me as "friends" should be.

We were no longer equals. Even though I saw them as equals still, it made them uncomfortable.

So in the end, I started to trust myself. I used my own kick ass mind as the grown, independent, adult woman I am and cut them out my life. It was hard, it was painful and I felt so full of shame and guilt. I felt these things as I had poor boundaries before and It felt alien to not be able to be friends with the many, many people I thought I had to save, fix and give up my life for- just to have friends, a purpose. I felt I did not deserve any better than to have people around me, who brought me down and sucked the life out of me.

They did not want me to succeed, to move on or see me happy. As long as I was serving them, I was the best friend in the world. When I started serving myself, oh how you see someone change and tear you down.

But alas, here I am clear minded, making the best decisions for me and my family.

Surrounded by beautiful friends, who are supportive and loving. I am listening to my intuition and growing more and more each day.

Permission

Permission from who?
Permission from you?
Permission for why?
Permission from only I...

Boundaries

Don't over step the line
The line from your boundary to mine.
Boundaries are there to keep us all safe and secure
Stop pushing and pulling, blurred boundaries no more.
Maybe I didn't make myself quite clear
My boundaries are important, did you not hear?

Better me

I am a better me without you
I am moving on, not feeling guilt for wanting new.
Growing and changing to better myself
Getting rid of drama that was bad for my health.
I hold no bitterness or remorse
I wish you well but we have run our course.
You took my kindness for a weakness
Drawing me in, playing on my meekness.
Yes this did hurt when I figured it out
I felt like a fool to not listen to my doubt.
Even though deep down I knew your intentions
I ignored my gut feeling and paid no attention.
In the games you played I was used as a pawn
But now I am winning with each new dawn.
I was disappointed to feel so deceived
To get caught up in the fakeness and lies you did weave.
The best thing I did was to show you the door
Because now I am happier, stronger, needing you no more.

LESSON NINE

Forgiveness

Some people can forgive, some people cannot and are unable too. I understand in given situations, it is extremely hard to forgive. I Have found forgiving those who have hurt me over the years, the most nourishing experience for my soul and being. It was not always easy for me to do that and have questioned many times, did I forgive just because I didn't want friction, confrontation?.

Does it then lead to being walked all over? The answer to these questions is YES.

Yes I did forgive far to many times and opened myself up to being walked all over, taken advantage of because I could not cope with the confrontation of not forgiving for any wrong doings of others.

The forgiveness I am talking about here, is for myself. For my own peace of mind.

I have forgiven my dad for the abuse he put us all through, forgiven my perpetrators, even the rapist. I have not done it for their sake though.

Bitterness and resentments eat away at your soul like a deep rooted disease.

Consuming all that is pure and kind, it hold you prisoner in your own mind. I forgave those that hurt me, because If I had not, they were still winning.

Still consuming my thoughts, feelings, my life.

They had already taken so much from me, I was not going to let them take any more.

There is a humility in being able to say sorry and ask for forgiveness, mean it, reflect and do it from a genuine place of love. Not just saying sorry because you have to, are forced to, being disingenuous for your own gain or needing to say it repeatedly for even being alive.

For so long sorry to me, was such an empty word, said by others for nothing to change, for their own gain.

Said by me to placate in fear.

It can be used far to much or not enough.

It can be said with love or aggression.

Used from hurting someone, used because you love someone

Said when it is meant, said when It is not.

If you say sorry and can really mean it, feel it deep within, it resonates so much clearer.

To forgive is powerful. To forgive, especially yourself is love.

Un-paused

You damaged me beyond all comprehension
Details to graphic, sordid to mention.
I don't understand how you can live with yourself?
Surely you must suffer, does it affect your mental health?
I wish you had it in you to hold yourself accountable
The sadness and sorrow you caused, insurmountable.
You never could say sorry for all the pain you caused
I can no longer wait, press play, life un-paused.

Letting go

My nightmares are what kept you alive
My dreams tried to win, they did strive.
I wish I could erase all traces of you
The distress you caused, I wish you knew.
If you knew, would it change a thing for me?- no
So I forgive for myself, it's time to let go.

New waters

All the pain, hurt and shame that I've felt
Felt from the hand I was dealt.
The hand I was dealt was one of sadness and tears
Tears that created oceans over the years.
Over the years the salt became too much
Became to bitter, toxic and such.
I swam and I swam to water anew
Anew where I could rest and forgive you.

Unearthed

I am unearthed
Unearthed from the soil
Soil rich with love and forgiveness
Forgiveness from the decay that was sown
From the decay, beautiful flowers have grown.
I am unearthed
Unearthed from the soil
Free and flourishing
Forgiveness is nourishing
I am unearthed.

Lesson ten

Finding

Can you really "find" yourself? Yes you can work on yourself, grow as a person if you choose. You can rebuild a new version of yourself, even enlighten yourself. Bringing out your potential.

All these things are already within you, they just need bringing out into the light.

I had wanted to find myself for a long time. I had a perception of what that should look like. Again I was wrong! Having finally found strength, courage, power that was already there, it was just hidden away. I just needed to believe in myself enough to recognise I was had all those things all along.

We all make mistakes, it is how we learn and grow. We are conditioned to believe that mistakes are awful, shameful experiences, when I fact we need them to learn.

Some situations I have found myself in have cause immense shame, guilt, embarrassment, hurt, pain and playing the victim.

I have been open and honest with the wrong people.

Telling my life story because I felt I had to, because then they'll like me better, feel sorry for me, like I felt sorry for them. Then I would blame myself and them when it all went wrong.

Refusing to look at my neediness and victimhood.

Being so nice to everyone, when I was screaming inside

"this is not what I want!"

Not having the courage to stand up for myself.

Being an empath impacts and magnifies this even more. Absorbing negative energies, feelings, thoughts and actions from lost souls. They fed and played upon my good nature.

Preyed on vulnerabilities.

Who would have though being kind and open could get you so hurt?

I guess I was never really honest. Even though I thought I was and portrayed myself that way. I was with my advice, opinions but in a sickly sugar coated way. I lied to myself constantly.

I lied I was happy.

I lied I had moved on.

I lied I was okay with my childhood.

Justifying a huge cocaine habit. Making excuses to why I had another partner, when I desperately needed to be on my own and have time to heal. I didn't recognise I needed time to recover. I would mask my problems by taking on everyone else's problems.

One big problem and one big ball of mess…

What do balls of wool usually do? Eventually unravel!

It has got me here today though. I have accepted my past has led me to the incredible path I am on now. I am able to use my knowledge and experiences to guide others in a more boundaried way. I have found my freedom from people pleasing and am assertive when it is called for.

I will no longer let anyone hand their life to me on a plate. I know I cannot help those, who don't wish to help themselves.

A helping hand with gentle guidance and direction is worth it's weight in gold. Letting go of your own ego, to listen, meet them half way. Draw on experiences, empathise but let them take control of their own solutions and choices.

Even if it is not what you would have chosen for them.

It does not matter, it is not your life. I found my relationship, especially with my brother started to improve dramatically when I adopted this attitude. When I found my boundaries, my compassion after rebuilding what we had lost for many years and for that I am eternally grateful.

However, if others actions do start to interfere with your life, have the courage and self-love to walk away. Love yourself enough, that now you are found, to set yourself and them free.

I am continuing my journey and am excited to go on learning, finding, discovering and most importantly accepting my truth.

As my truth stands right now, it's pretty damn good!

Dear future self

Once upon a time there was a girl, a girl who felt she never belonged. Always felt different, she has extraordinary experiences from a young age. Experiences that could not be explained, did not happen to anyone else and were at times unnerving.

Her life was full of sadness and she was scared. This girl did not feel worthy and wondered what must be wrong with her for her world to be this way…. WAS there anything wrong with her? Did she even want to be here? Was she ever going to feel safe, loved, good enough?

It turns out as the years went by she found herself in some very dangerous situations, doing things she did not always want to do just to fit in, be accepted, to feel….loved.

She dreamed of escaping, of meeting a prince to whisk her away and live happily ever after, she soon came to realise that fairy tales were indeed just, fairy tales. There was no magical prince to come and save her from herself.

She ended up being the one who rescued everyone else. Who lived to serve and please, even those that certainly did not deserve or warrant it. All the while this did not make her bitter towards life, she just did not understand why it kept happening time and time again. There must be something wrong…..Right? Something she was being punished for?.

Then one day she started to realise there was nothing wrong with her, but it was going to take A LOT of work on herself to fix herself. To undo the lifetime of hurt caused by others – men and women, young and old, she had to do this for herself, by herself.

So the journey began… a wonderful journey of growth, change and of spiritual enlightenment. She started to be true to her calling. It was terrifying, she was scared and uncertain. After all she spent so long denying what was right for her, not trusting what she knew was always there in her soul….Intuition.

A gift so ingrained in her very being, over thousands of years, spanning millennia.

She was lucky enough to be built of strength, a resilience in her bones, to find courage to make huge life changes. Moving towards people who helped restore her faith in human kind, who started to raise her up and believe in her. With their belief, so her own in herself began to grow. She started to trust herself, make better choices, began to heal wounds that had been open and raw for as long as she could remember. She began to find who she was, what she liked, what she enjoyed with a new found freedom from fear.

She has started to build confidence, not shying away from using her voice, for speaking her truth and what she feels passionate about.

She connects with the universe, with mother nature. Worships the Goddess' – she is at one with the stars, she is from the stars …… she knows that now.

Full of wonder for the skies, full of intrigue, wanting to learn all she can.

She loves to learn, acquire as much knowledge as possible.

She is incredible, successful, happy, content, full of love for herself. She has peace, shows compassion and kindness always. She shows no judgement and listens to herself and others. She has found her soul group – like minded, amazing people. People who deserve her time, friendship and love.

She knows when the time is right she will meet the one who is worthy of her heart, one of whom she can be an equal and share her life with.

She has been on the most incredible journey and the best is still to come, just as I planned it to be.

I am she, she is I and I am PROUD TO BE SHE xxx

Acknowledgements

I have so many people to thank for all their unwavering support on my writing journey.

Firstly I want to thank my babies for keeping me focused and giving me a reason to beat addiction and become a better version of myself, so I can be a better mum to you both. I love you with all my heart and more.

Next comes my parents. My mum and dad for all their encouragement, their support to get me through some of the roughest times in my life. Always there to listen and guide when I needed it the most.

To my dad and step mum for us building a strong relationship.

I give thanks to my brother for giving me 2 wonderful nieces and him and Sarah for giving me a nephew and for allowing us to grow into what we should have always been, a brother and sister.

I have some super special friends that are more like family to me and have stuck by my side through thick and thin, showing unwavering support when i have been full of doubt. Giving me honest feed back about my writing, being there to bounce ideas off of and listening to me when I've needed them too and of course an huge thanks to my beta readers.

Annie, Zoe, Craig, Emma, Emma, Tracy, Debs, Michelle, Donna, Von, Betty, Vicky, Vicky and Ben.

You are all truly wonderful and I love you xx

Also, a special mention to my coach, Steph as without her guidance and patience I would never have even started to unpick my trauma or had the courage to reach for my dreams.

Jennifer Leigh Pezzano , who I connected with as her beta reader, your advice, guidance and wisdom through the whole journey has been amazing and I am so grateful being a self published author yourself.

Last but not least, to all my passed loved ones. The kick ass women I looked up to – nanny, auntie Lyn, Teri and Traze. Also my Nanny Nancy who I may not have known long but you made my mum who she is and I am like her, so like you.

Always in my heart xxx

Printed in Great Britain
by Amazon